NEYMAR

BY ERIN NICKS

WORLD'S
GREATEST
SOCCER PLAYERS

SportsZone

An Imprint of Abdo Publishing
abdobooks.com

abdobooks.com

Published by Abdo Publishing, a division of ABDO, PO Box 398166, Minneapolis, Minnesota 55439.

Printed China
092019
012020

Cover Photo: J.E.E./Sipa/AP Images
Interior Photos: Andre Penner/AP Images, 4, 10, 12, 15; Silvia Izquierdo/AP Images, 6, 16; Kyodo/AP Images, 8–9; Eugene Hoshiko/AP Images, 18; Manu Fernandez/AP Images, 21; Siu Wu/AP Images, 22; Christian Liewig/Sipa/AP Images, 24; Miguel Schincario/AFP/Getty Images, 27; Francois Mori/AP Images, 28

Editor: Patrick Donnelly
Series Designer: Craig Hinton

Library of Congress Control Number: 2019941994

Publisher's Cataloging-in-Publication Data

Names: Nicks, Erin, author.
Title: Neymar / by Erin Nicks
Description: Minneapolis, Minnesota : Abdo Publishing, 2020 | Series: World's greatest soccer players | Includes online resources and index.
Identifiers: ISBN 9781532190650 (lib. bdg.) | ISBN 9781644943441 (pbk.) | ISBN 9781532176500 (ebook)
Subjects: LCSH: Silva Santos Júnior, Neymar da, 1992- (Neymar)--Juvenile literature. | Paris-Saint-Germain (Soccer club)--Juvenile literature. | European football--Biography--Juvenile literature. | Soccer players--Biography--Juvenile literature. | Professional athletes-- Biography--Juvenile literature.
Classification: DDC 796.3340922--dc23

TABLE OF CONTENTS

THE GOLDEN GOAL

Neymar kissed the ball and placed it on the penalty spot, knowing the entire country of Brazil was waiting and watching. The hopes and dreams of his fellow Brazilians were riding on his next kick.

It was August 20, 2016. Neymar's Brazil team was facing Germany in the gold-medal match of the 2016 Olympics. This wasn't just any other championship game, though. It was being played in Rio de Janeiro, Brazil, the host city of the Olympics that year. And just two years earlier in the World Cup, which was also played in Brazil, Germany

Neymar prepares to take his turn in the shootout at the 2016 Olympics.

BRASIL
11
10
Rio2016
Rio2016
2016

had dealt the host team an embarrassing 7–1 defeat in the semifinals.

Neymar had missed that match due to injury. So the gold-medal match against Germany gave Brazil and its captain a chance for redemption. Neymar opened the scoring off a free kick, but Germany tied it early in the second half. After 90 minutes of regulation time and two 15-minute extra time periods, the score remained tied 1–1. The winner would be determined by a penalty shootout.

Each country had scored on its first four penalty kick attempts. Then it was time for Brazil's goalkeeper, Weverton, to come up with a huge play. He stopped the last shot by Germany's Nils Petersen. This left the door open for Brazil and its captain to win the match and the gold medal on the next kick.

Neymar rejoices after his first-half goal put the home team on top.

The Rio home crowd held its breath waiting for the kick. Neymar started to run at the ball, but then he suddenly slowed, trying to fake out keeper Timo Horn. Neymar then sped up again and kicked the ball. Horn dived to Neymar's left, but his guess proved wrong. Neymar went the other way, flicking the ball into the top right-hand corner of the net. Brazil had won the gold medal.

Neymar immediately fell to his knees and wept as the Brazilian fans yelled out in celebration. The proud South American nation had waited a long time for Olympic gold. Brazil had lost in the finals in 1984, 1988, and 2012. Neymar's big kick had finally placed them on top of the podium, and the victory had come on Brazilian

Tensions were high as Neymar made the final kick of the shootout.

100% JESUS
Rio2016

soil. Neymar said afterward that it was one of the best things that had happened in his life.

Neymar has gained a reputation as one of the greatest soccer players in the world. He is the third player in history to score at least 60 goals for the soccer-loving nation of Brazil. Pelé scored 77 goals and Ronaldo scored 62. With his speed and amazing foot skills, Neymar is one of the planet's most exciting players to watch.

SOCIAL GIANT

As one of the most famous soccer players in the world, Neymar has a large presence on social media. His Facebook fan page has more than 60 million likes. He is also one of the most popular people on Instagram, with more than 122 million followers. That puts him in the top 10 in the world among Instagram users.

Neymar proudly displays his gold medal after Brazil won a thrilling Olympic final.

S.F.C.
SEARA
SEARA

CHAPTER
TWO

EARLY LIFE

The soccer superstar known as Neymar was born as Neymar da Silva Santos Júnior on February 5, 1992, in Mogi das Cruzes, Brazil. Neymar Sr., a former professional soccer player, encouraged his young son to take up the sport. Neymar worked on his skills by playing in the streets of his hometown and in informal games with his friends.

In 2003 the family moved to Santos. Once there, Neymar joined the youth academy of Santos FC, where the great Pelé once played. As he grew, Neymar became more confident as a soccer player. He was extremely fast

Neymar was just a teenager when he began playing for the Santos FC senior team.

NICKNAMES

One of Neymar's earlier nicknames was "Juninho," which means "Little Junior" in Portuguese. More recently he has been called "O Joia," or "the Jewel."

with great reflexes, which helped him control the ball much quicker than his opponents could.

Neymar made his debut with Santos in 2009 when he was 17 years old. He soon developed a reputation as an exciting goal scorer. In 2010 he was nominated for the Puskás Award. It goes to the international player who scores the most impressive goal each year. During a game against Santo Andre, Neymar took a pass on the left wing. He faked out two Santo Andre players before heading to the net. One defender slid across the ground, trying to block Neymar's shot. Instead, Neymar hesitated again, pushing the ball back to his right before taking a shot. The ball went between the legs of a fourth defender and past

Neymar quickly became a fixture in the Santos lineup.

SEARA
NETSHOES

NETSHOES
NETSHOES
NETSHOES

the diving goalkeeper. It was a spectacular goal for the teenage superstar.

But Neymar wasn't just there to score goals. He wanted to win trophies. In 2011 Santos faced off against Peñarol of Uruguay in the final of the Copa Libertadores—the South American club championship. Neymar opened the scoring off a pass from defensive midfielder Arouca. Neymar ran to the left side of the Peñarol box and sent a rocket past keeper Sebastián Sosa's near post. Neymar leaped into the air in triumph as his teammates gathered around him to celebrate.

Santos went on to win 2–1. It was the first time the club had won the title since 1963. Neymar was named the South American Footballer of the Year that year, as well as in 2012. Soon it became clear that he was ready to take his game to the next level.

Neymar, *left*, celebrates with his teammates after he scored a goal against Peñarol in the 2011 Copa Libertadores final.

BRASIL
10

CHAPTER THREE

CLUB AND COUNTRY

In 2013 Neymar left South America to face the world's best players in Europe. He made the move to Spain and signed a five-year contract with FC Barcelona. However, his Brazilian roots would always be important to him. He continued to represent his home country in many international events.

Neymar played for Brazil at home in the 2013 Confederations Cup. He scored four goals in the tournament, which Brazil went on to win. His biggest goal came in the match against Japan. During the third

Neymar scores Brazil's first goal in a 2013 Confederations Cup match against Japan.

minute, a teammate stopped a long cross with his chest. The ball landed on the ground at the top of the penalty area, leaving it in a perfect position for Neymar. He played it off a half volley, firing it past keeper Eiji Kawashima and into the net. Brazil eventually beat Japan 3–0. At the end of the tournament, Neymar was awarded the Golden Ball for being the tournament's most valuable player.

In 2014 Neymar represented Brazil again, this time at the World Cup. His country was also hosting the event, which made the stakes even higher. Brazil started strong. Neymar's offensive talent was on display for everyone to witness. He scored four goals in five matches. But in the quarterfinals against Colombia, Neymar broke a bone in his back in a big collision. Brazil won, but Neymar's tournament was done. Brazil's offense suffered without him, and they suffered a humiliating defeat to Germany in the semifinals.

Neymar was injured on this hard foul by Colombia's Juan Zuniga in the 2014 World Cup quarterfinals.

18
10
10

Neymar joined Suarez, *left*, and Messi, *right*, in Barcelona's star-studded lineup.

Neymar was able to recover from his injury, and soon the awards started piling up, both for him and for Barcelona. In 2015 Neymar and Barcelona captured their second continental treble by winning three big trophies.

They took first place in La Liga, the top Spanish league. They won the Copa del Rey, a yearlong single-elimination tournament in Spain. And Barcelona came out on top in the Champions League, which determines the best club team in Europe. Barcelona was stacked with offensive superstars. Neymar was part of a high-scoring trio alongside Lionel Messi and Luis Suárez. Fans combined the initials of the stars' last names, and the scorers became known as "MSN."

FINDING THE NET

Neymar was a major part of Barcelona's offensive success during his time with the club. He scored 105 goals in 186 games in four years with Barcelona.

But Neymar was soon to be on the move again. He was ready to take on the role of main man at another one of Europe's top clubs.

PARIS
SAINT-GERMAIN
Fly
PARIS
NEYMAR JR
10
LFP
LFP
ooredoo

CHAPTER
FOUR

HEADING TO PARIS

Paris Saint-Germain (PSG) is one of the richest clubs in the world. After winning four straight titles in Ligue 1, France's top league, PSG came up empty in 2017. Looking to give its offense a boost, the club purchased Neymar's contract in the summer of 2017.

Neymar is a popular player and is recognized around the world. When he was 19 years old, he signed an 11-year deal with Nike. SportsPro named him its most marketable athlete for both 2012 and 2013. In 2016 ESPN named Neymar the fourth most famous athlete in the world,

Neymar was excited for his 2017 debut with Paris Saint-Germain.

NEYMAR IN THE MEDIA

In 2017 Neymar made his acting debut alongside Vin Diesel in *XXX: The Return of Xander Cage*. That same year *Time* magazine listed him as one of its "100 Most Influential People."

behind Cristiano Ronaldo, basketball star LeBron James, and Messi. The move to Paris would give him an even higher profile.

Neymar also has worked to help others and give back to the community through different types of charity work. The *Instituto Projeto Neymar Jr.* opened in 2014 in Praia Grande, Brazil. More than 2,400 children attend the institute. Many of these children live in poverty. The institute uses sports to encourage and promote healthy living. Neymar often plays in charity matches called *Amigos de Neymar* in his native Brazil to raise food donations for needy families.

Neymar debuted for PSG on August 13, 2017, and he scored in his first match. It was a sign of things to come.

Neymar poses with his son Davi Lucca and female players at a charity tournament in Brazil in 2018.

Neymar scored 28 goals in 30 matches in his first season in France, including 19 in 20 league matches. That same season he helped PSG capture a domestic treble: Ligue 1, the league cup, and France's national cup.

On May 4, 2019, Neymar scored his 50th goal in 57 games with PSG. His club was playing in a Ligue 1 match against Nice, and Neymar was awarded a penalty shot after teammate Angel Di Maria was knocked down by Nice's Patrick Burner. Neymar took a stutter step, trying to catch keeper Walter Benitez off guard. He then sent a strike from 12 yards into the left side of the net. The home crowd at Parc des Princes immediately began to chant and cheer for their star, whom they hoped would bring multiple trophies back home to Paris.

Transfer rumors swirled in the summer of 2019. Many observers thought Neymar was headed back to Barcelona or perhaps was on his way to Real Madrid. In the end, he stayed in Paris. Neymar scored a brilliant goal in stoppage time to beat Strasbourg 1–0 in his first game back. Though his future in Paris remained uncertain, Neymar continued to show that his talent was never in question.

Neymar holds the Ligue 1 championship trophy, which he helped PSG win in each of his first two seasons with the club.

GLOSSARY

free kick
An unguarded kick awarded to a team after an opponent's foul.

half volley
Kicking the ball out of midair on a bounce.

marketable
Having skills or attributes that are attractive to people looking to buy something.

native
Associated with a person's place of birth.

near post
The goalpost closest to the player shooting the ball.

penalty area
The box in front of the goal where a player is granted a penalty kick if he or she is fouled.

penalty spot
The white dot in front of each goal where the ball is placed before a penalty kick is taken.

podium
A small platform on which a person may stand to be seen by an audience, as when making a speech or receiving a medal.

reflexes
Automatic reactions that happen without thinking.

treble
Winning three major competitions in one season.

MORE INFORMATION

BOOKS

Billioud, Jean-Michel. *Soccer Stars: Meet 40 Game Changers*. London: Wide-Eyed Editions, 2018.

Jökulsson, Illugi. *Messi, Neymar, and Suárez: The Barcelona Trio*. New York: Abbeville Press, 2016.

Killion, Ann. *Champions of Men's Soccer*. New York: Philomel Books, 2018.

ONLINE RESOURCES

To learn more about Neymar, please visit **abdobooklinks.com** or scan this QR code. These links are routinely monitored and updated to provide the most current information available.

INDEX

ABOUT THE AUTHOR

Erin Nicks is from Thunder Bay, Ontario. She has written about sports for newspapers and websites for the past 20 years. She currently lives in Ottawa, Ontario.